rodrigo y gabriela

9 DEAD ALIVE

T0056688

WISE PUBLICATIONS
part of The Music Sales Group

London / New York / Paris / Sydney / Copenhagen / Berlin / Madrid / Hong Kong / Tokyo

Published by
Wise Publications
14-15 Berners Street, London W1T 3LJ, UK.

Exclusive distributors:
Music Sales Limited
Distribution Centre, Newmarket Road,
Bury St Edmunds, Suffolk IP33 3YB, UK.

Music Sales Pty Limited
Units 3-4, 17 Willfox Street, Condell Park,
NSW 2200, Australia.

Order No. AM1009602
ISBN 978-1-78305-737-5
This book © Copyright 2014 Wise Publications,
a division of Music Sales Limited.

Music arranged by Matt Cowe.
Music engraved by Paul Ewers Music Design.
Edited by Adrian Hopkins.

Printed in the EU.

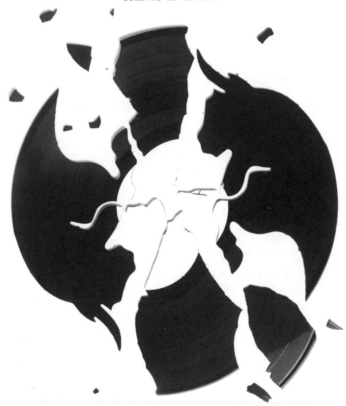

Your Guarantee of Quality:

As publishers, we strive to
produce every book to the highest
commercial standards.

Particular care has been given to specifying
acid-free, neutral-sized paper made from pulps which
have not been elemental chlorine bleached.

This pulp is from farmed sustainable forests and was
produced with special regard for the environment.

Throughout, the printing and binding have been
planned to ensure a sturdy, attractive publication
which should give years of enjoyment.

If your copy fails to meet our high standards,
please inform us and we will gladly replace it.

www.musicsales.com

The Soundmaker 9

Torito 19

Sunday Neurosis 30

Misty Moses 38

Somnium 48

FRAM 58

Megalopolis 70

The Russian Messenger 79

La Salle des pas perdus 88

Guitar Tablature Explained 4

Guitar tablature explained

Guitar music can be explained in three different ways: on a musical stave, in tablature, and in rhythm slashes.

RHYTHM SLASHES: are written above the stave. Strum chords in the rhythm indicated. Round noteheads indicate single notes.

THE MUSICAL STAVE: shows pitches and rhythms and is divided by lines into bars. Pitches are named after the first seven letters of the alphabet.

TABLATURE: graphically represents the guitar fingerboard. Each horizontal line represents a string, and each number represents a fret.

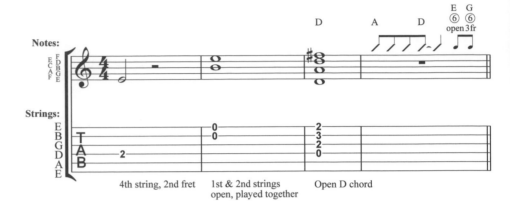

4th string, 2nd fret   1st & 2nd strings open, played together   Open D chord

Definitions for special guitar notation

SEMI-TONE BEND: Strike the note and bend up a semi-tone (½ step).

WHOLE-TONE BEND: Strike the note and bend up a whole-tone (full step).

GRACE NOTE BEND: Strike the note and bend as indicated. Play the first note as quickly as possible.

QUARTER-TONE BEND: Strike the note and bend up a ¼ step

BEND & RELEASE: Strike the note and bend up as indicated, then release back to the original note.

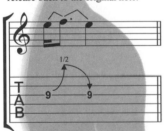

COMPOUND BEND & RELEASE: Strike the note and bend up and down in the rhythm indicated.

PRE-BEND: Bend the note as indicated, then strike it.

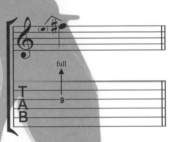

PRE-BEND & RELEASE: Bend the note as indicated. Strike it and release the note back to the original pitch.

HAMMER-ON: Strike the first note with one finger, then sound the second note (on the same string) with another finger by fretting it without picking.

PULL-OFF: Place both fingers on the note to be sounded, strike the first note and without picking, pull the finger off to sound the second note.

LEGATO SLIDE (GLISS): Strike the first note and then slide the same fret-hand finger up or down to the second note. The second note is not struck.

MUFFLED STRINGS: A percussive sound is produced by laying the first hand across the string(s) without depressing, and striking them with the pick hand.

NATURAL HARMONIC: Strike the note while the fret-hand lightly touches the string directly over the fret indicated.

PICK SCRAPE: The edge of the pick is rubbed down (or up) the string, producing a scratchy sound.

PALM MUTING: The note is partially muted by the pick hand lightly touching the string(s) just before the bridge.

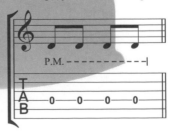

SHIFT SLIDE (GLISS & RESTRIKE) Same as legato slide, except the second note is struck.

Special percussion techniques

The following notation is used in this book to try and illustrate the unique percussive playing techniques used by Rodrigo Y Gabriela. These are particularly relevant to the rhythmic accompanying parts performed by Gabriela. Experiment with these techniques, and study the original recordings, to emulate her sound:

Percussive hit, either on the bridge (for a low sound), or on the fretboard (for a sharper sound). This is performed with varying degrees of muting with the fretting hand to create different effects.

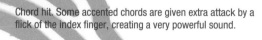

Chord hit. Some accented chords are given extra attack by a flick of the index finger, creating a very powerful sound.

Muted stroke. The strings are muffled by the fretting hand, and then a played to produce a percussive sound with upstrokes and downstrokes of either the fingers or thumb.

Hit to body of the guitar with knuckles or fingers (either of the fretting hand for accents or both hands for more extended percussive sections).

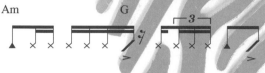

This is a typical example of the parts that Gabriela plays, combining hits with accented chords and muted notes. Different combinations of upstrokes and downstrokes using the index and middles fingers, and thumb are used to execute these kind of figures. Typically, alternating upstrokes and downstrokes are used. Triplet figures are played by a downstroke with the fingers followed by a further downstroke with the thumb and lastly an upstroke with the thumb.

Percussive sections: extended figures like this are performed by either drumming on the body of the guitar with the fingers and knuckles (Gabriela) or drumming below the soundhole with the fingers (Rodrigo).

Additional musical definitions

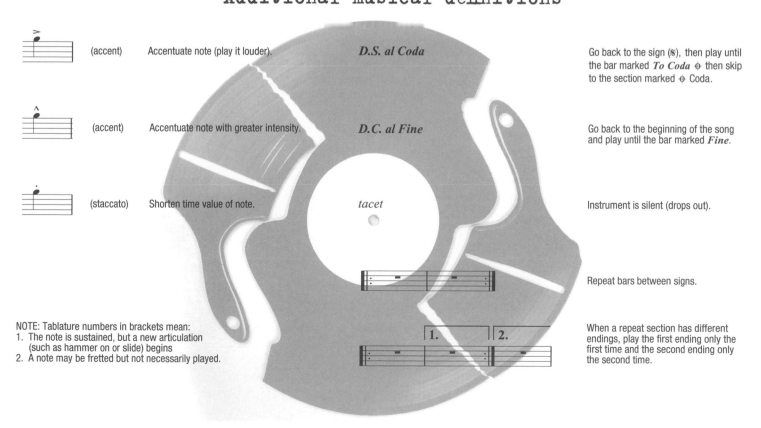

(accent) Accentuate note (play it louder).

D.S. al Coda — Go back to the sign (𝄋), then play until the bar marked **To Coda** ⊕ then skip to the section marked ⊕ Coda.

(accent) Accentuate note with greater intensity.

D.C. al Fine — Go back to the beginning of the song and play until the bar marked **Fine**.

(staccato) Shorten time value of note.

tacet — Instrument is silent (drops out).

Repeat bars between signs.

1. **2.** — When a repeat section has different endings, play the first ending only the first time and the second ending only the second time.

NOTE: Tablature numbers in brackets mean:
1. The note is sustained, but a new articulation (such as hammer on or slide) begins
2. A note may be fretted but not necessarily played.

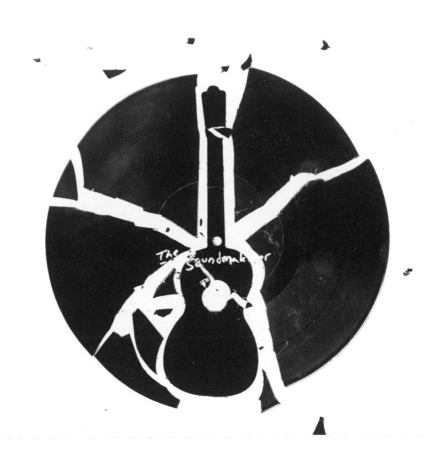

The Soundmaker

Music by Rodrigo Sanchez & Gabriela Quintero

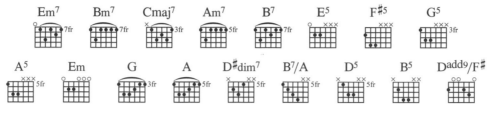

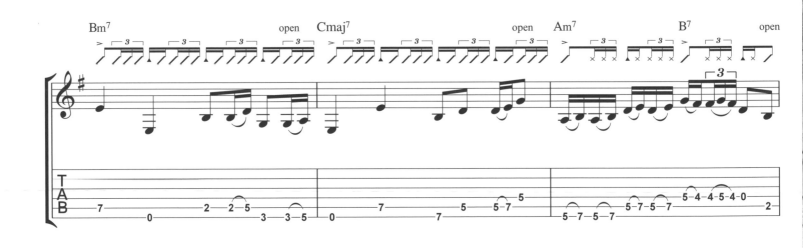

13

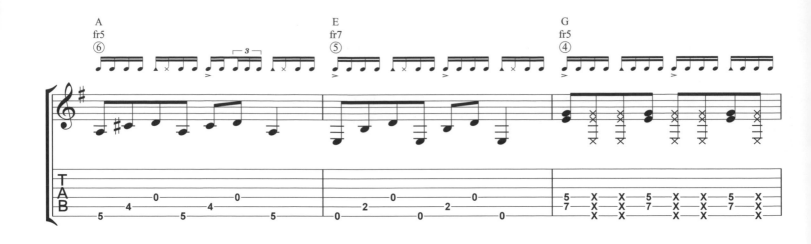

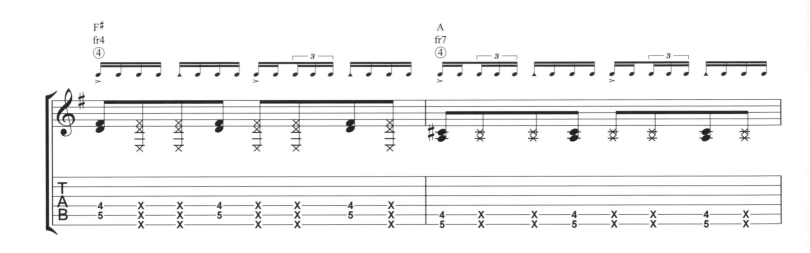

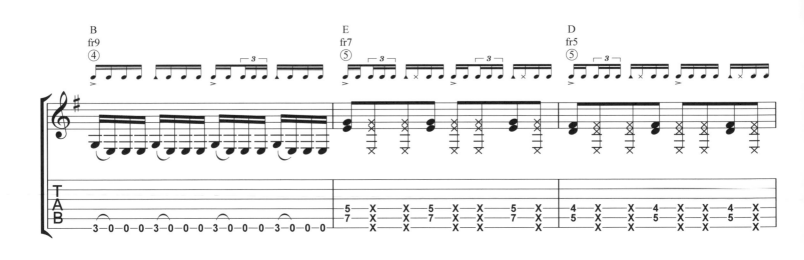

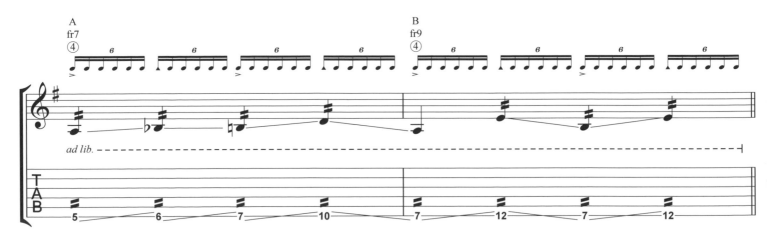

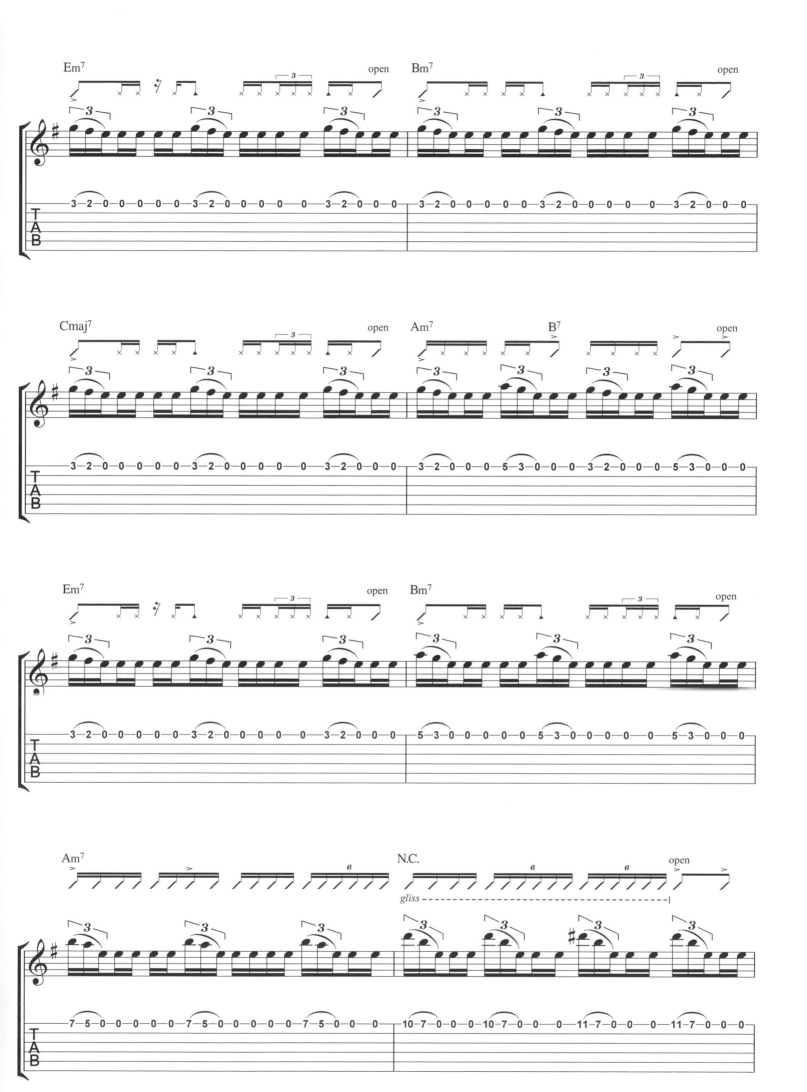

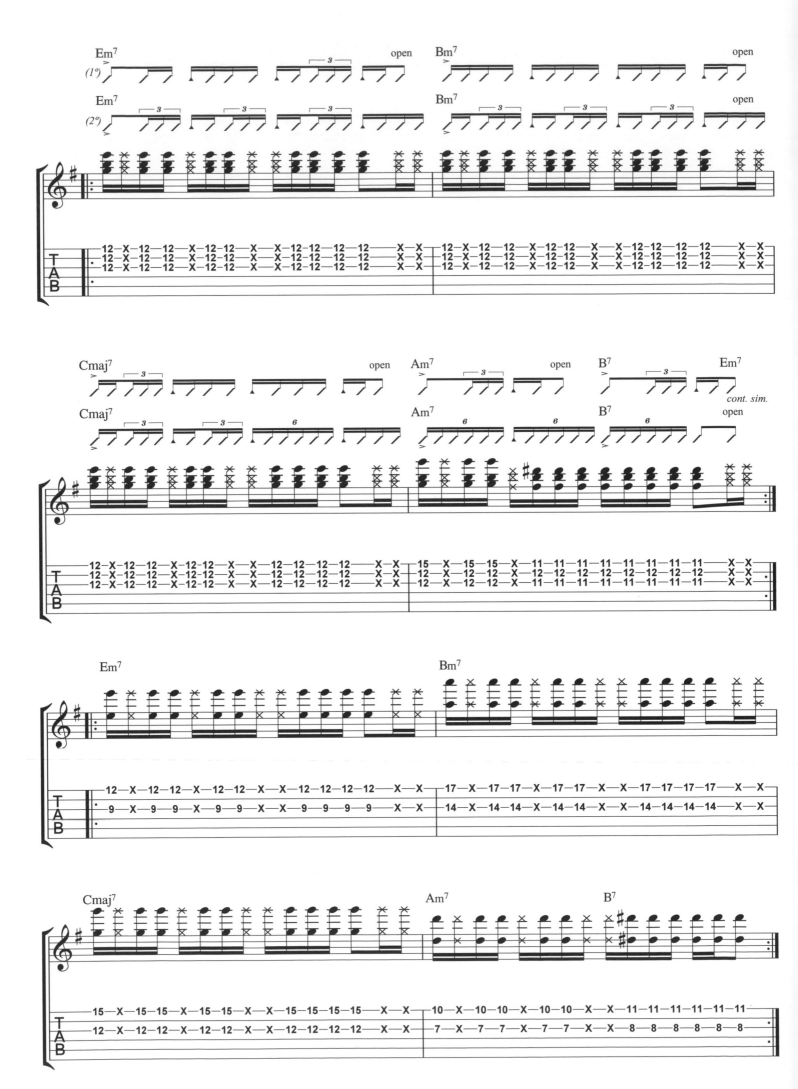

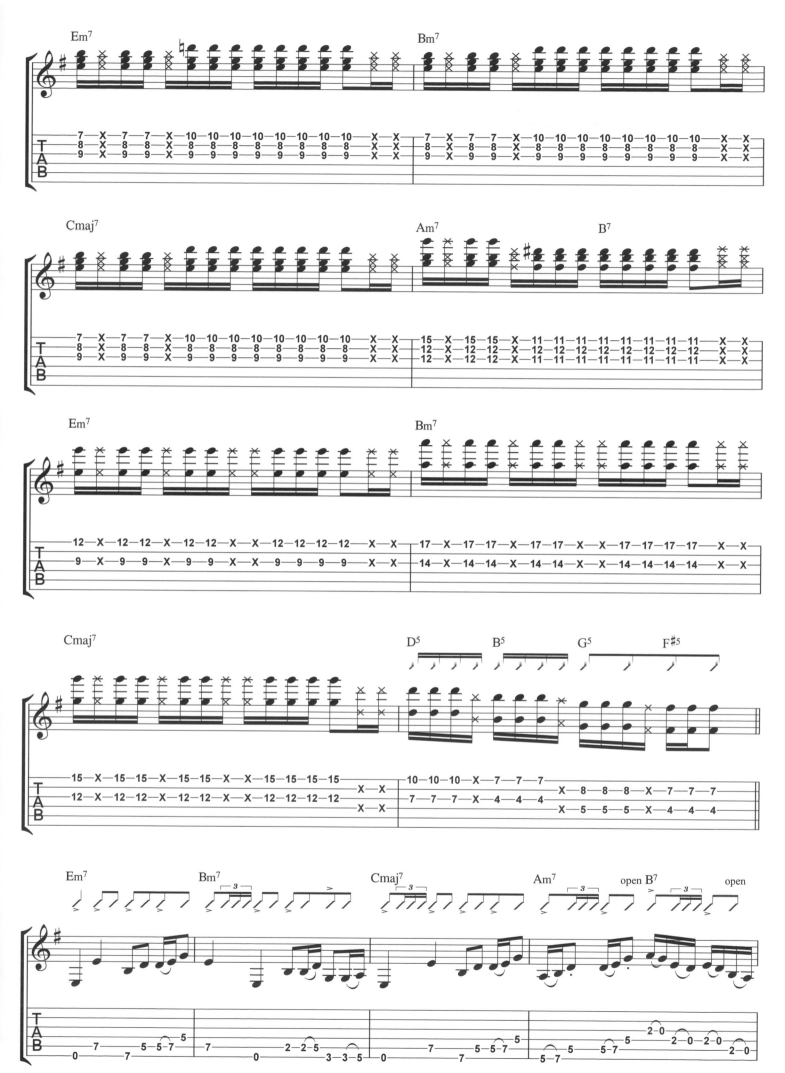

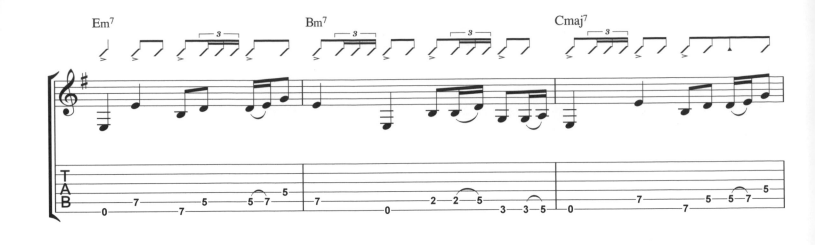

Torito

Music by Rodrigo Sanchez & Gabriela Quintero

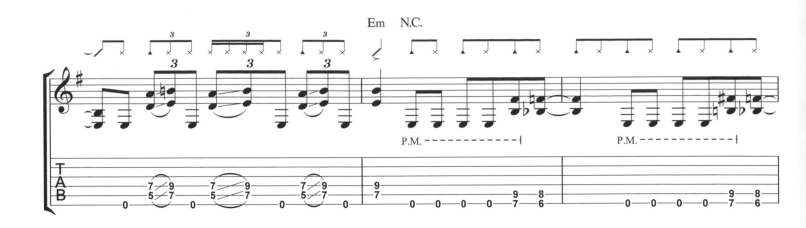

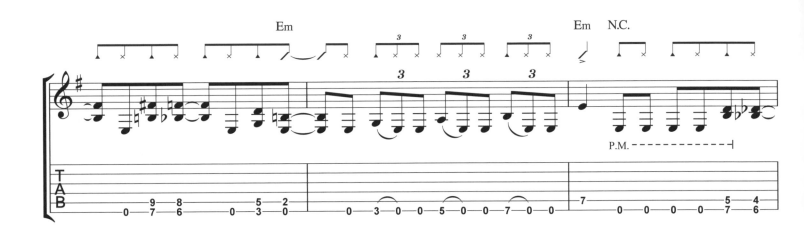

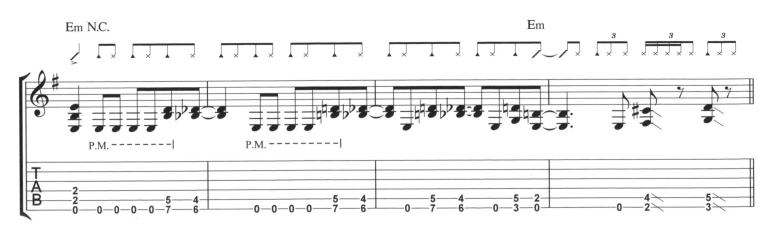

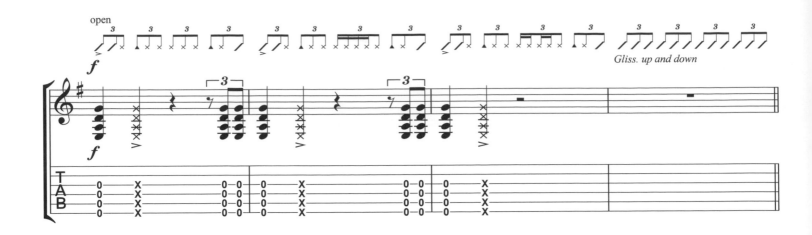

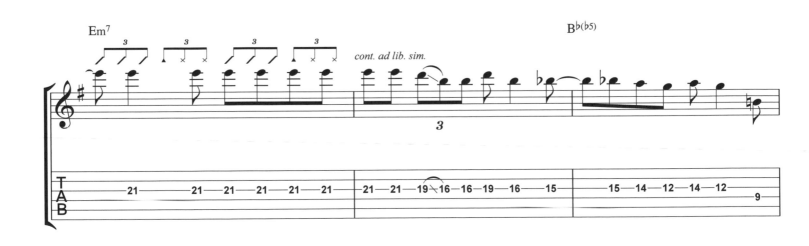

Sunday Neurosis

Music by Rodrigo Sanchez & Gabriela Quintero

* softly with R.H. palm

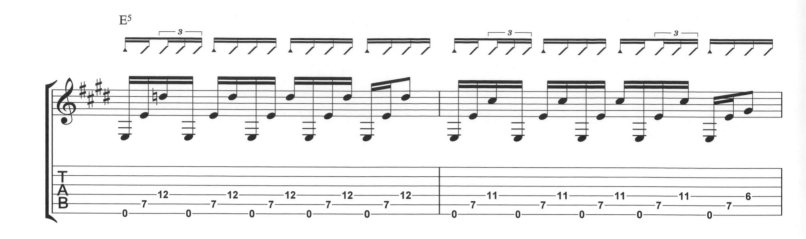

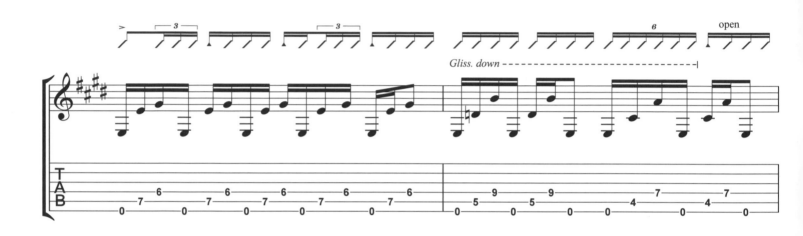

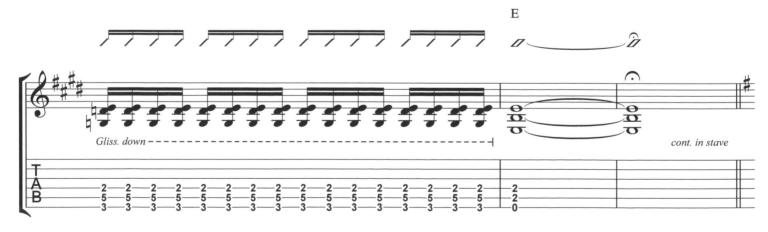

Misty Moses

Music by Rodrigo Sanchez & Gabriela Quintero

Somnium

Music by Rodrigo Sanchez & Gabriela Quintero

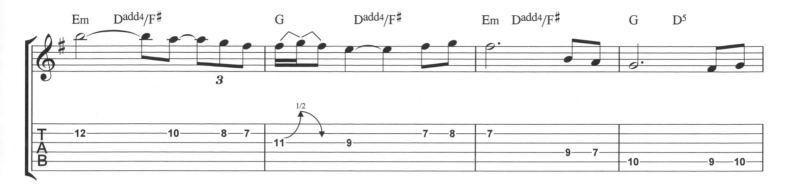

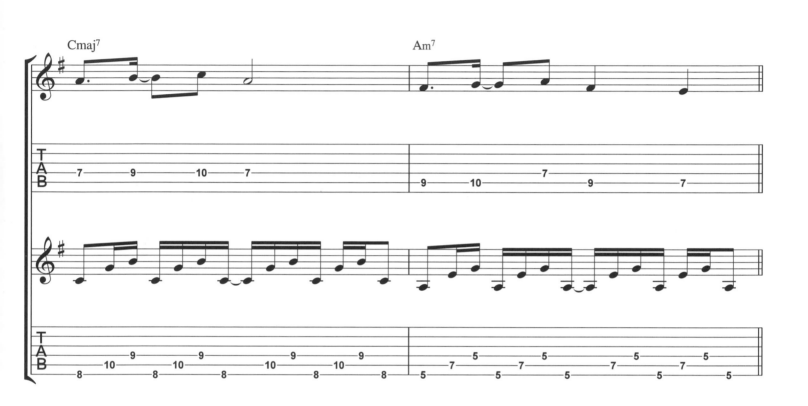

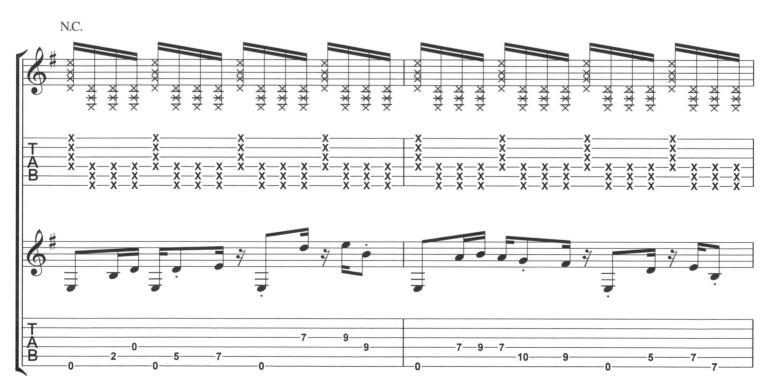

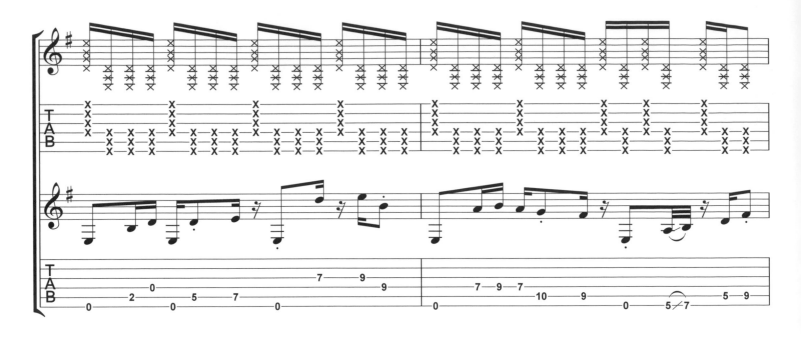

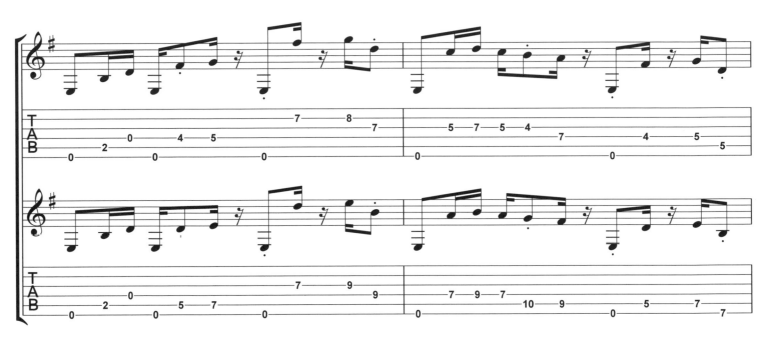

Gtr. 1 *cont. in slashes*

50

53

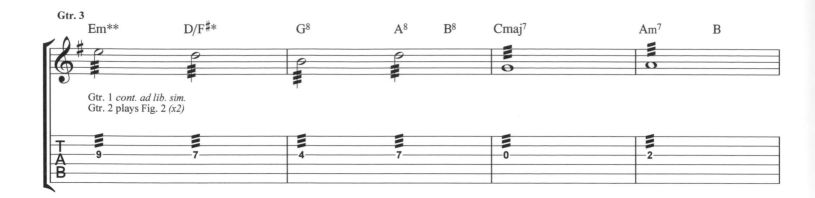

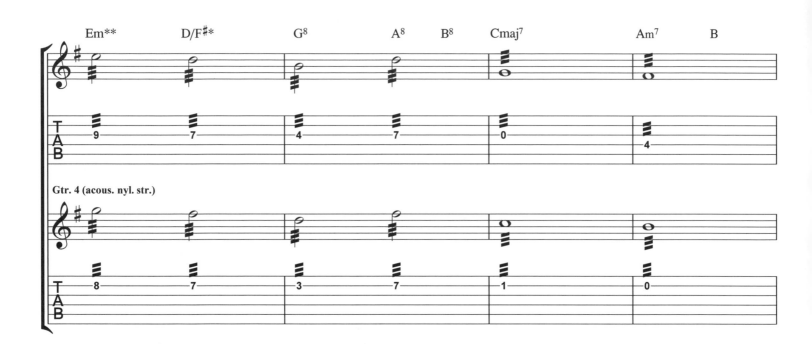

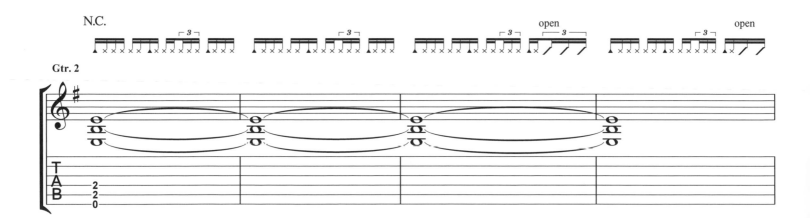

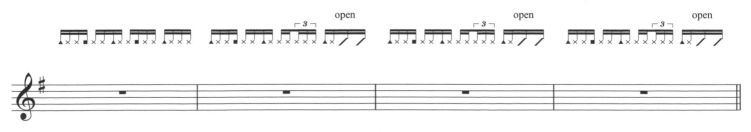

FRAM

Music by Rodrigo Sanchez & Gabriela Quintero

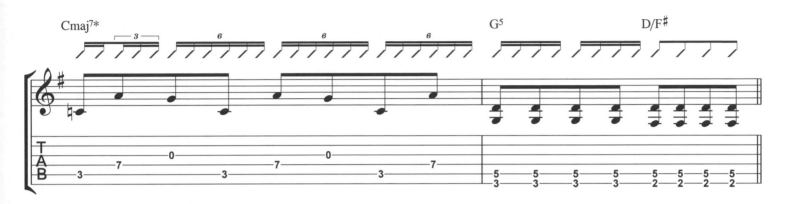

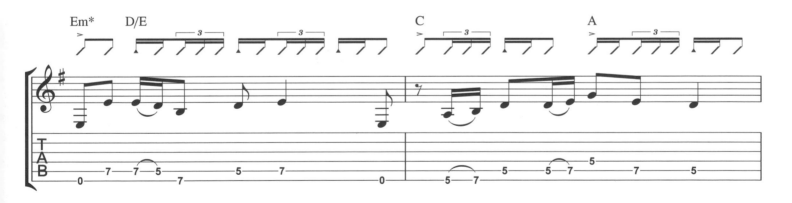

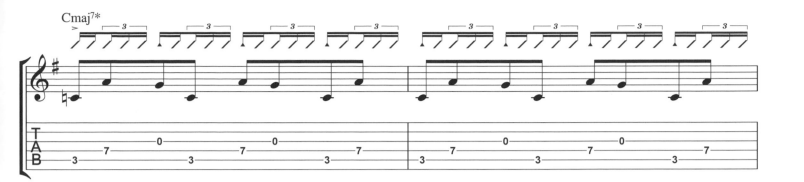

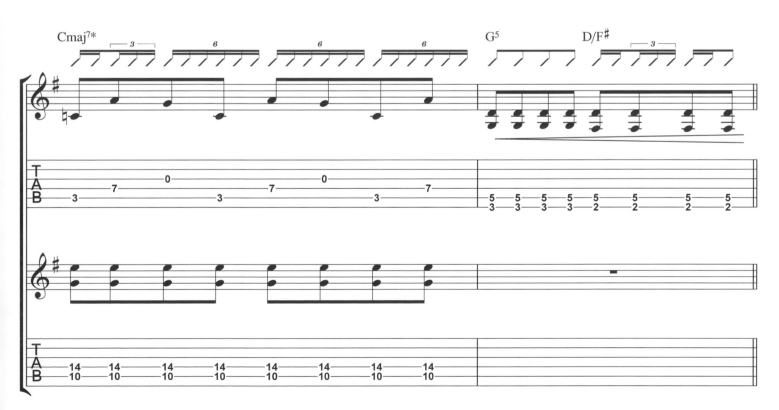

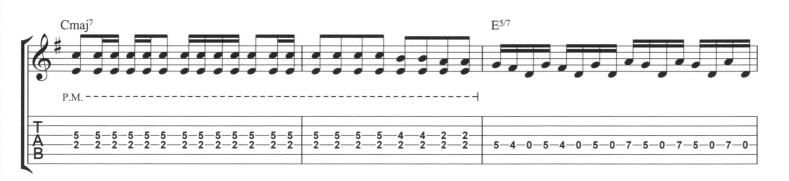

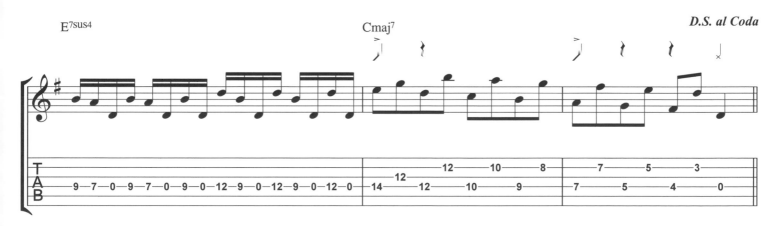

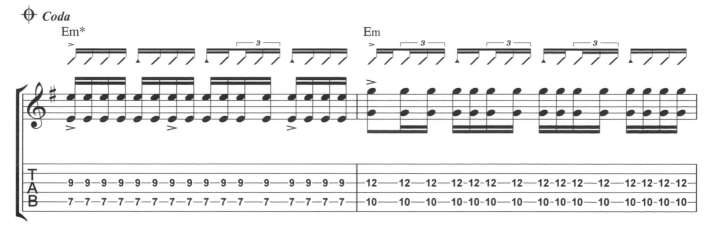

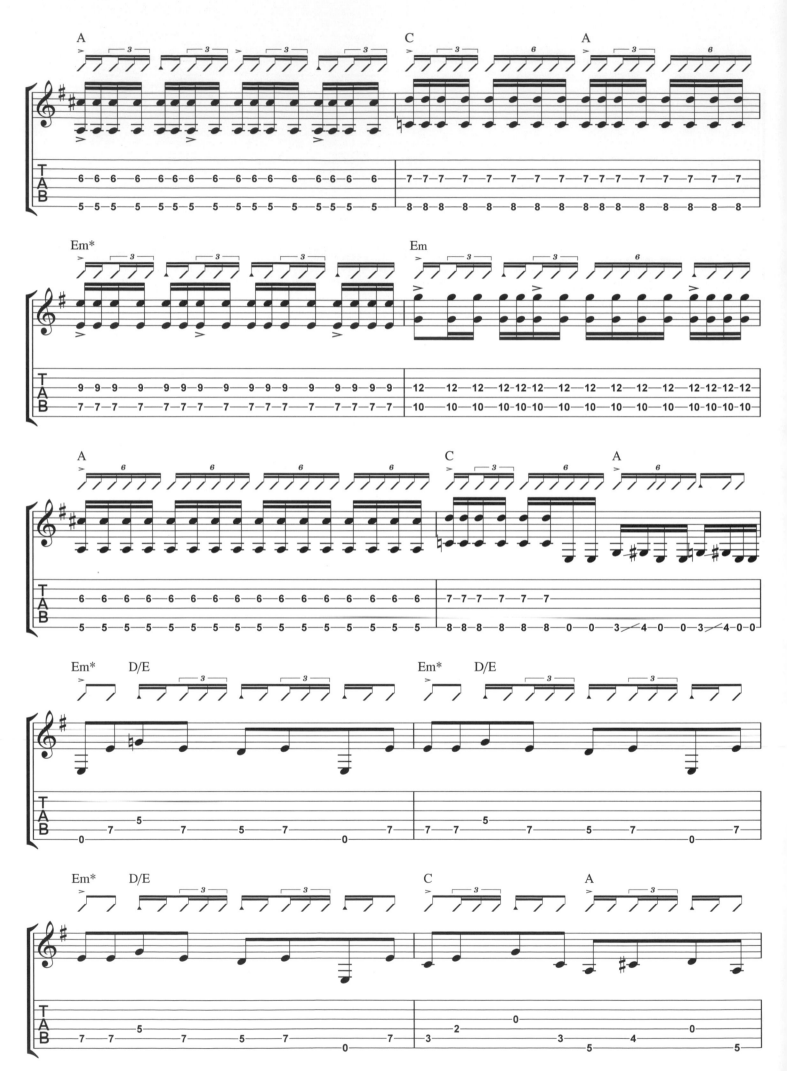

Megalopolis

Music by Rodrigo Sanchez & Gabriela Quintero

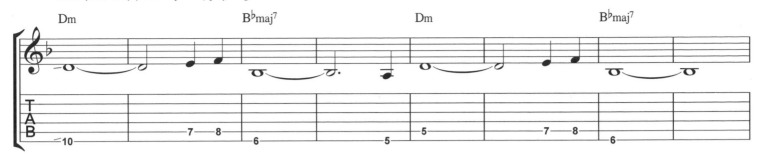

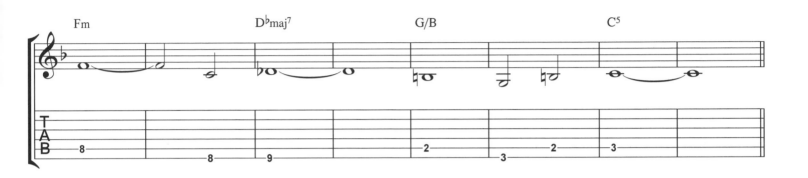

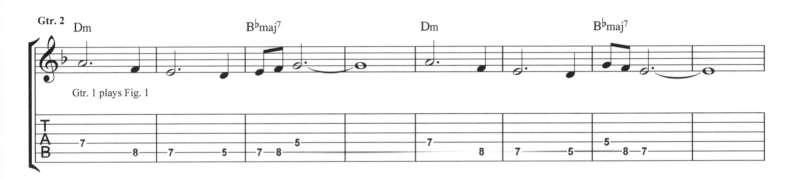

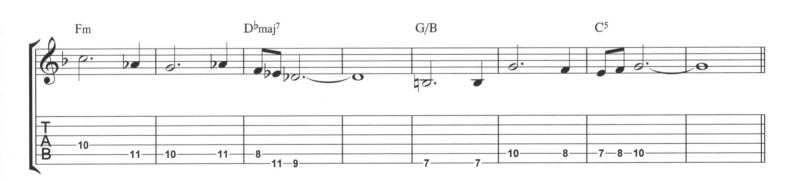

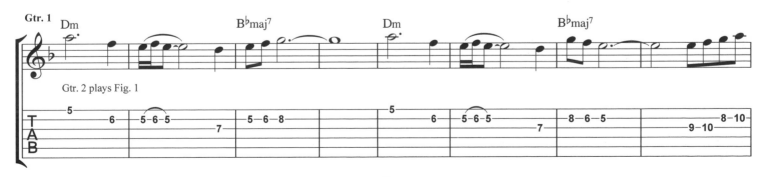

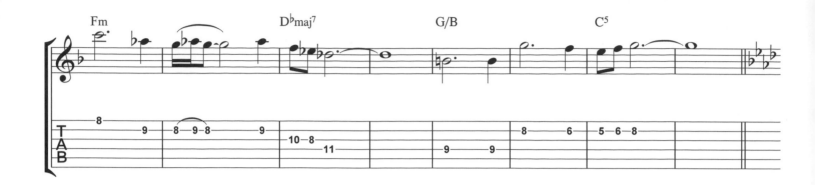

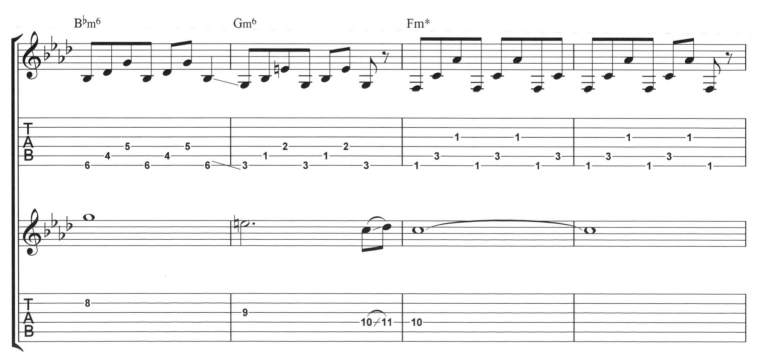

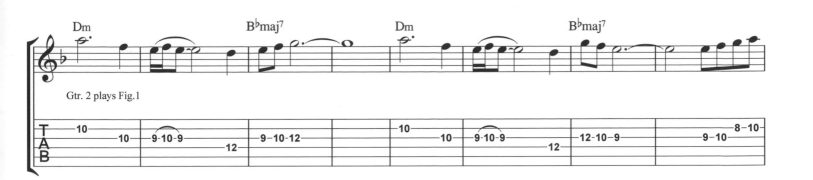

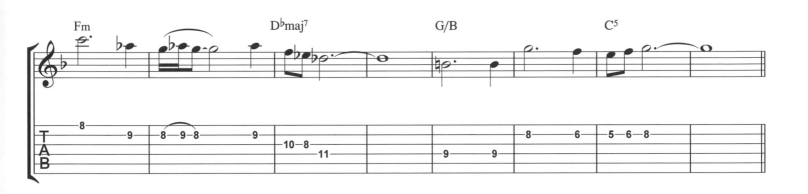

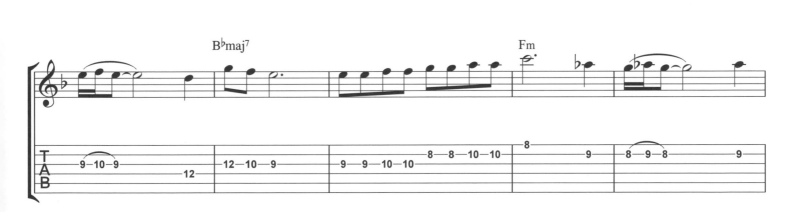

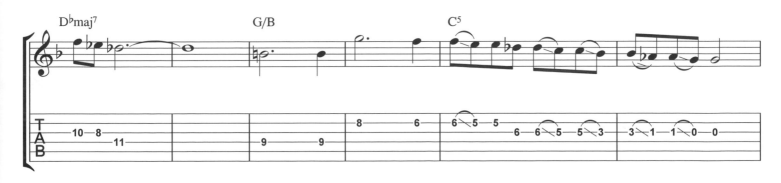

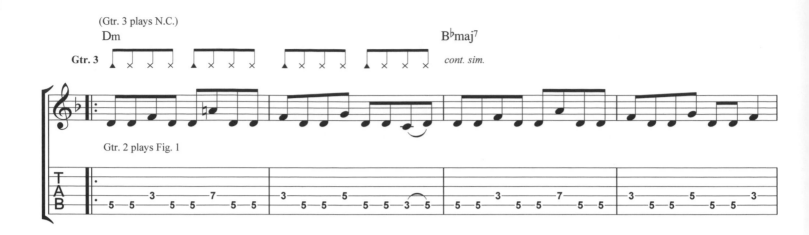

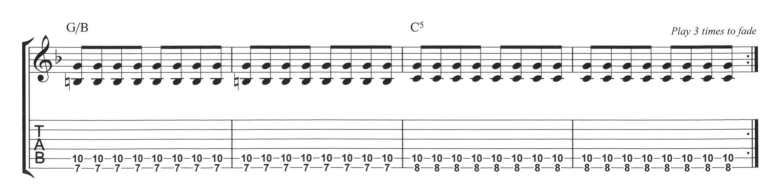

The Russian Messenger

Music by Rodrigo Sanchez & Gabriela Quintero

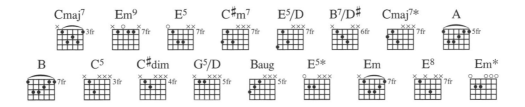

cont. in slashes

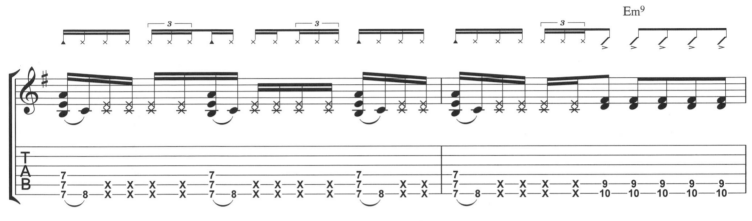

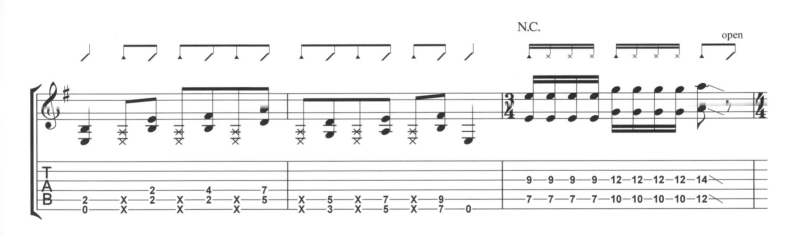

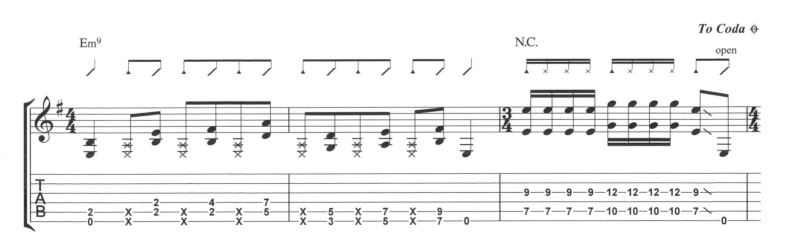

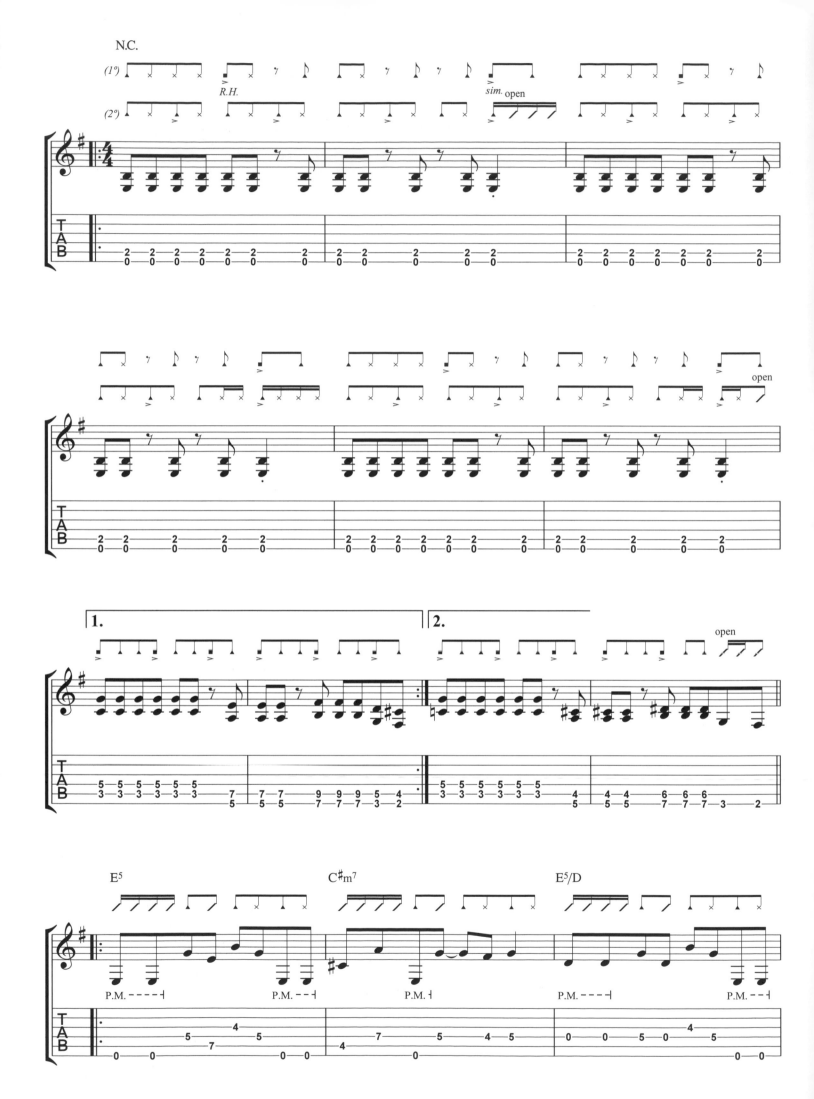

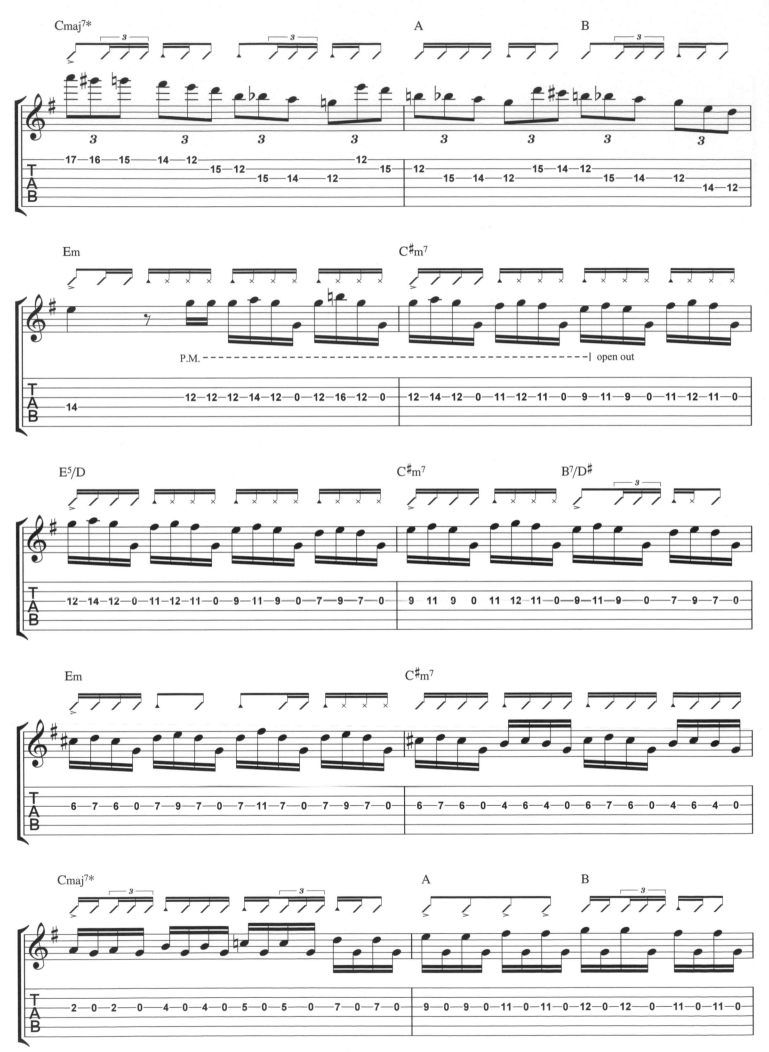

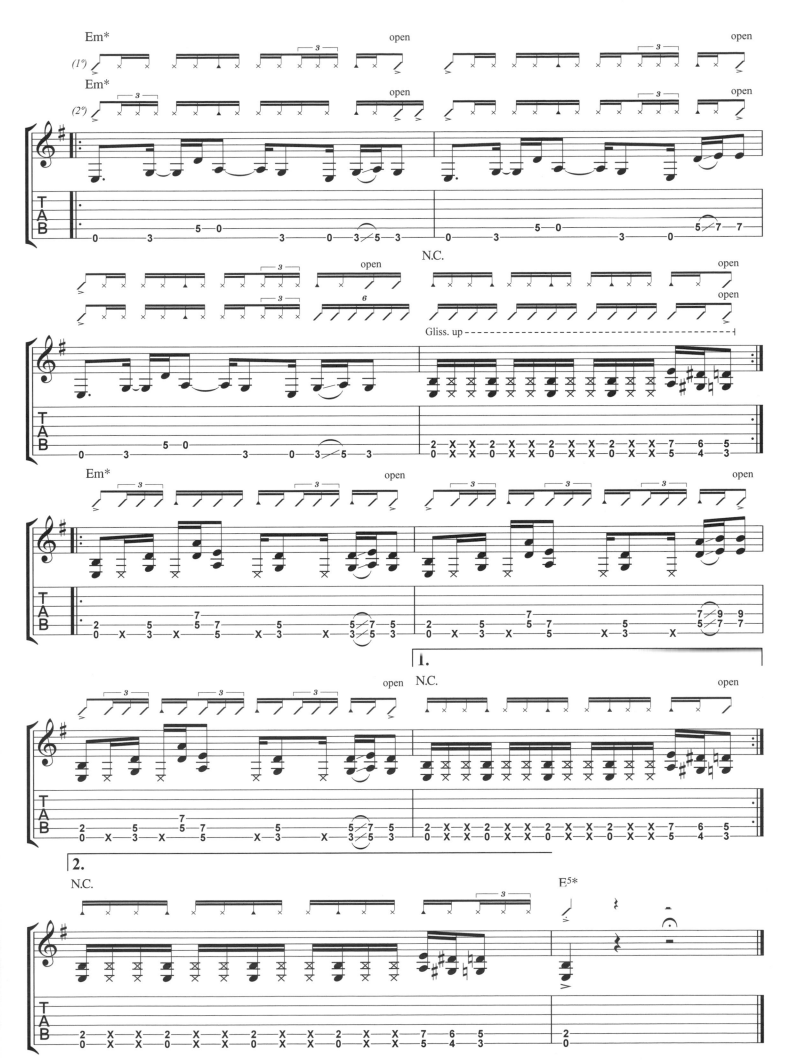

La salle des pas perdus

Music by Rodrigo Sanchez & Gabriela Quintero

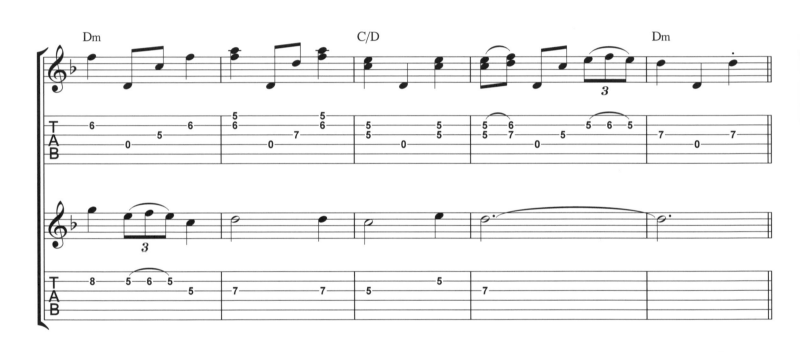

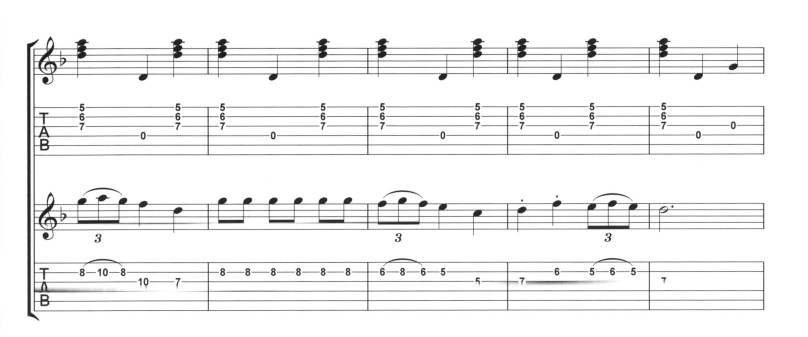

2 3 4 5 6 7 8 9

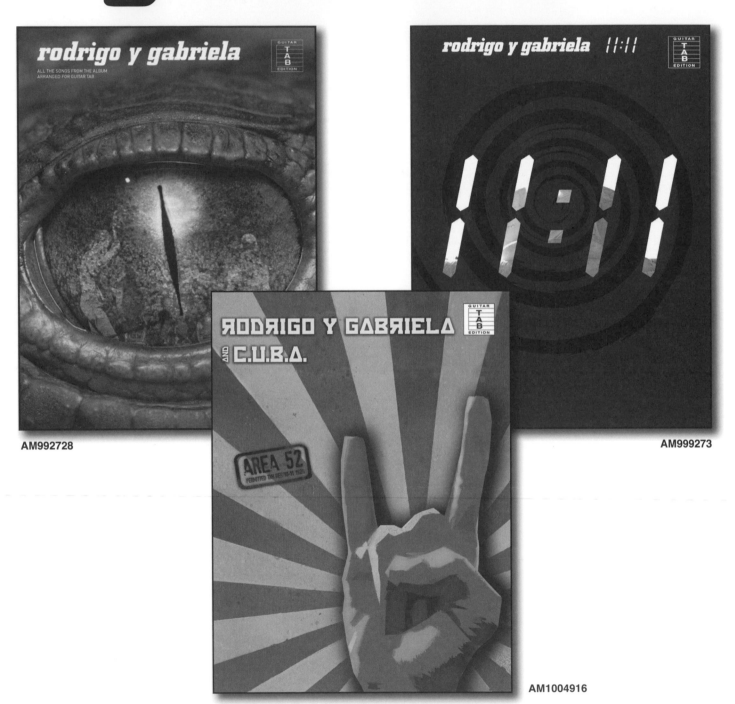